The Seasons

William B. Rice

Consultants

Sally Creel, Ed.D.
Curriculum Consultant

Leann Iacuone, M.A.T., NBCT, ATC
Riverside Unified School District

Jill Tobin
California Teacher of the Year
Semi-Finalist
Burbank Unified School District

Image Credits: p.5 (top) Wayne Lynch/
agefotostock; p.17 Stouffer Productions/
agefotostock; pp.6–7 Gay Bumgarner/Alamy;
p.16 William Leaman/Alamy; p.9 Dimitri Vervitsiotis/
Getty Images; p.15 (top) Donald M. Jones/
Getty Images; pp.4, 11 Petegar/iStock; pp.20–21
(illustrations) Janelle Bell-Martin; all other images
from Shutterstock.

Library of Congress Cataloging-in-Publication Data

Rice, William B. (William Benjamin), 1961- author.
  The seasons / William B. Rice; consultants, Sally Creel,
Ed.D., curriculum consultant, Leann Iacuone, M.A.T., NBCT,
ATC, Riverside Unified School District Jill Tobin, California
Teacher of the Year Semi-Finalist, Burbank Unified
School District.
     pages cm
  Summary: "During the summer it is warm outside.
During winter it is cold. This is because there are
different seasons. Can you name the other two
seasons?"— Provided by publisher.
  Audience: K to grade 3.
  Includes index.
  ISBN 978-1-4807-4569-8 (pbk.)
  ISBN 978-1-4807-5059-3 (ebook)
1. Seasons—Juvenile literature. I. Title.
  QB637.4.R525 2015
  508.2—dc23
                                    2014013157

Teacher Created Materials

5301 Oceanus Drive
Huntington Beach, CA 92649-1030
http://www.tcmpub.com
ISBN 978-1-4807-4569-8

Table of Contents

Changing Earth

There are many changes on Earth during the year. Plants change. Animals change. The air, sky, and clouds change.

New plants change as they grow during the year.

Lion cubs play and get stronger.

Young animals grow up.

5

Seasons change, too. They change from spring to summer to autumn (AW-tuhm) to winter. Then, it is spring again.

spring

summer

Cycle of Seasons

Is there a first season? No, the seasons go in a **cycle** (SAHY-kuhl). There is no beginning or end.

autumn

winter

Season to Season

Plants grow in spring. It may rain. The air gets warmer. Many animals are born.

Rain helps plants grow in spring.

New Life

New plants and animals often begin to grow in spring.

9

In summer, the air is warm. Plants grow bigger. They may grow fruit. Baby animals grow up.

These lambs grow in summer.

These flowers bloom in summer.

In autumn, the air gets cool. Rain may fall again. Many plants are ready to **harvest**. Most plants stop growing. Young animals are nearly grown.

Fall

Autumn is also called *fall*. Leaves turn colors and then fall in autumn.

Pumpkins are ready to harvest in autumn.

In winter, it is cold. Sometimes it snows or rains. Some plants have died. The leaves are gone from many trees.

It snows in many places in winter.

Eat Up!

There is less food in winter. So animals try to eat and store plenty of food during spring, summer, and autumn.

These trees lost their leaves.

Some animals **hibernate** (HI-ber-neyt) in winter. Birds may **migrate** (MAHY-greyt), or move to a place in the world where it is warmer.

These geese migrate to a warmer place for winter.

This bear hibernates in winter.

Changing Seasons

Time moves forward, and so do the seasons. One season becomes the next. One day it is spring, and before you know it, spring is back again!

New plants grow in spring.
The cycle keeps going.

Let's Do Science!

What happens when seasons change?
Try this and see!

What to Get

- ⭕ 4 twigs
- ⭕ crayons
- ⭕ glue
- ⭕ paper
- ⭕ scissors

What to Do

1 Glue each twig to the middle of a sheet of paper. Each twig will be a tree trunk.

2 Write a season at the top of each paper.

3 Use paper or crayons to make a tree for each season. Add branches, leaves, pine cones, flowers, or animals to show the seasons.

4 How are the trees alike? How are they different?

Glossary

cycle—a pattern in a full circle, with no beginning or end

harvest—to pick food from plants

hibernate—to sleep during winter

migrate—to move from one area to another at different times of the year

seasons—the four different times of year marked by changing weather and length of day

Index

23

Your Turn!

Changing Seasons

Look at the trees and plants outside. Do the trees have leaves? What color are the leaves? What does the air feel like? Can you tell what season it is by what you see and feel?